Don't Manage…

Coach!

Martin Klubeck & Michael Langthorne

Publisher: Createspace Independent Publishing Platform

This book is really for all of the workers, staff, and employees who have to suffer because their boss thinks they are a resource to be managed instead of a valued team member who should be coached

May all those in "management" learn to be better coaches

About the Authors

Martin Klubeck

Martin is a recognized leader in Organizational Development – specifically Metrics, Vision Setting, and Professional Development Planning. Martin has helped organizations design, create, and use meaningful metrics programs for over 20 years. His ability to take the complex and simplify it makes him a highly sought after teacher and consultant. His energy and concern for the success of others makes him a top notch speaker.

Martin is currently the author of four books; "Why Organizations Struggle So Hard to Improve So Little: Overcoming Organizational Immaturity" (ABC Clio, 2009), "Metrics: How To Improve Key Business Results" (Apress. 2011), Planning and Designing Effective Metrics (Apress 2014) and The Professional Development Toolbox (2015). He holds a Master's degree in Human Resources Development from Webster University, a Bachelor's degree in Computer Science from Chapman University and an Associate's degree in Instructional Technology from the Community College of the Air Force.

Martin's compulsion to help others has led to the creation of his company MK Knowledge Builders, a weekly motivational newsletter for vision setters, numerous publications and presentations, and now this book. You can contact Marty through his website (mkknoweldgebuilders.com), LinkedIn, or Twitter.

Michael Langthorne

 Following several years in television news production, Michael worked at the University of Notre Dame where he served in many roles in IT. He has published articles in numerous professional journals since 1978, and was the distinguished recipient of a 1992 award for Facilities Design from the International Communication Industries Association.

Michael is a co-author (with Martin Klubeck and Donald Padgett) of "Why Organizations Struggle So Hard to Improve So Little" (2009, ABC/Clio), editor of several other business books, and the author of the novel "Navigating Infinity" (2013).

Over the years Michael has consulted with a variety of businesses, colleges and organizations, and has presented at conferences in the United States, Ireland, France and Canada.

Contents

Introduction

Why Martin wanted to write this book

You can be a better manager! And it doesn't take extraordinary effort. All it takes is a change in perspective – a new way to look at your role.

In Marcus Buckingham and Curt Coffman's excellent book, "First Break All the Rules," we find the clear explanation that the front-line manager is the most important factor in an employee's level of work satisfaction. It's not the amount of pay. It's not the ergonomic furniture, the proximity to good housing, or parking. It's all about the relationship between the manager and the worker.

From our own experiences, we fully concur with this analysis. This critical relationship was the primary reason for writing our book. We know the manager is critical to the employee's satisfaction and to the company's success.

Buckingham and Coffman spend a good portion of their book sharing the ways great managers (few in number) differ from the masses. The best managers hire for talent rather than skills or experience. The best managers set expectations and define the right outcomes rather than laying out the procedures. The best managers motivate people by building on their strengths; not fix weaknesses. The best managers "find the right fit for each person, not the next rung on the ladder."

"First Break All the Rules" is a phenomenal best seller. It's constantly on the top of the sales lists for book distributors. There are tons of other good books which also urge managers to change their ways. There are loads of articles written on the subject. There are courses, classes, workshops and seminars. There is no shortage of people trying to get managers to do it differently. So why is the inability of managers to bring out the best in their workers still a rich target area?

Why with all of this great advice aren't we being overrun by awesome managers?

Why with all of this training, guidance, and tools aren't managers seen as the savior of the American corporation (as they could and should be)? What's keeping us from embracing all of these great suggestions? Even the advent of a new focus on metrics (performance measures especially) and a renewed focus on professional development hasn't led to better management.

It's obviously not enough. Nothing so far has broken past the powerful barrier, the wall that separates great managers from the rest. We need a wakeup call for managers! We need a jolt, a spark! We need something that will actually work. We need a way to transform well-meaning managers into well-performing ones.

We come bearing good news.

We believe we've found the answer. Managers need a model to follow. A blueprint. Not just what has worked for others…but why it works. A clear, understandable and easily copied way to succeed.

Most times the answer isn't a complicated formula. Most times it's a simple change in viewpoint, a new way of looking at the problem.

A new paradigm. A new way of doing things. An easy to understand, easy to remember, way to change. A philosophy based on proven ideas and methods – not theory, but practical reality. And a paradigm that is attractive – a chance to redefine in a positive light who and what management is.

The things the "best" managers do is exactly what any "good" coach does! And while there are mediocre coaches out there – the difference is that what we propose isn't just doing what the good coaches (and best managers) do. We want you to stop managing at all...and start coaching. Because even the mediocre coach sees their job differently than a manager does. A mediocre coach would still be an improvement over most managers.

Sports is more than a metaphor in this case – it's a real-life, practical model to follow. And that's what we suggest. Not to "think" and "act" like a coach...but to truly become a coach. Rather than read books on how to manage, read books on how to coach. Rather than emulate the best managers, do what they do and emulate the best coaches!

This book is meant to be nothing short of judo for the soul of managers, flipping the stale components of "managing" on their backs while lifting off the mat a new role, a completely changed role – the Coach.

Why Michael wanted to write this book

Since the "Great Recession" of 2008, it's been an employer's market. Unemployment and under-employment were seemingly becoming systemic, causing millions of people who had jobs to fear for those jobs, to fear to even try changing jobs (mainly because of the old adage, "last in, first out"). What does it mean to be working, or trying to obtain work, during an employer's market? In the majority of instances it means individuals putting in far more than 40 hours of work per week while being paid less (in current dollar value) than they may have earned ten years before. It means individuals frequently covering not one, but two or three positions every day due to worker terminations and attrition. It means individuals living with daily stress of losing their jobs. The obvious outcome? Those individuals work harder than ever before, while trying to maintain some shred of positivity about the future.

But what tends to follow an economic downturn? A gradual uptick. Productivity improves, supply and demand re-balance, and the consumer begins buying again. And when the consumer buys, businesses want to increase production to meet demand. Suddenly they realize they cannot increase production and maintain quality customer service without hiring more workers. That appears to be the situation today – hopeful signs and real numbers indicating economic improvement. So what will long time workers and new hires expect and demand as they see businesses struggle to find qualified workers? When the economy begins to shift from an employer's market to an employee's market, wages increase.

Obviously wages are bedrock to a functional society, but the dollar figure alone on paychecks doesn't buy employee loyalty or passion. Nor does it necessarily buy improved worker productivity. The business environment itself is either the chemical that invigorates employees, elevating their desires for success, or it's the poison in the well that eats away at morale, enthusiasm and loyalty. And for most workers, the business environment is determined (consciously or accidentally) from the top down, by the leadership they might not see very often and by the managers they see every day. An organization's culture is a synthesis of that top-down business environment combined with employee response. And managers are the group designated to manage employee "response" by managing performance.

Unfortunately, "managing" has gotten a bit of a bad rap in the past few years. Hundreds of business books tout leadership instead. "Set the vision. Lead by example." Lofty sentiments for the typical workplace where someone high up in leadership sets production goals and sales goals and then tells the managers to "Make It Happen!" And in order to make it happen, managers have by and large fallen into the trap of status quo – track what workers do, how much of it they do, and just focus on this quarter because there's no time to search the horizon for new opportunities.

Martin and I are in complete agreement: this book is meant to be nothing short of judo for the soul of managers, flipping the stale components of "managing" on their backs while lifting off the mat a new role, a completely changed role – the Coach.

Don't Manage…

8   Don't Manage...

What does it mean to manage and what's right about it?

---

*"The man who complains about the way
the ball bounces is likely the one who
dropped it."*
– Lou Holtz

What does a manager actually manage? Supposedly resources, which includes materials, budget and people. Does the manager manage people's time? Their behavior? Their output? Or is it all-encompassing? Does he or she manage "performance"?

---

*"The general feeling is, if you don't treat
everyone the same you're showing
partiality. To me, that's when you show the
most partiality, when you treat everyone
the same. You must give each individual the
treatment that you feel he earns and
deserves, recognizing at all times that
you're imperfect and you're going to be
incorrect oftentimes in your judgment."*
– John Wooden.

On his way to becoming general manager, Fred managed a restaurant kitchen. He was in charge of a staff of 12, and in charge of keeping the kitchen and all its equipment in clean and proper condition. That meant Fred had a budget for replacing a few pots and pans and knives each year (or for repairing a fridge or stove every five years), and that he assigned the shifts each staff member (including the chef) would work. He assigned who handled specific food prep, cooking functions, and clean-up functions. So apparently Fred mostly managed by assignment. But wait – he also had to make sure everyone on staff fulfilled their assignments. So Fred had to spend time observing. And while observing he noted how well each staff member performed his or her role, how well they worked individually and as a team. If meals were not prepared correctly, in a timely manner, or were returned by customers, he had to quickly find out what was wrong and either correct the situation with the poor performer or send him home. If he had to do that, he had to get someone to fill in (possibly even himself if no one else was available).

So part of managing is observing performance and taking action if performance is below standards.

Fred hired staff, assigned work, and monitored performance. Fred rewarded staff who exceled, reprimanded (in some way) staff who were sub-par, and terminated employment for staff who remained sub-par after taking steps to help them improve. He also had to explain to staff what the company standards were (in general) and any additional specific standards he personally had.

Let's say Fred had a fantastic year with 12 high quality staff – they fulfilled their assignments very well, and did them with a smile. They delivered excellent meals, gained compliments from customers, and always let Fred know if they perceived any developing problems or circumstances that might hinder meeting standards. That's it, life was great. Fred didn't even need to come by the restaurant each night! Well, he did in fact always put in at least 8 hours a day at the restaurant, but they were easy hours, and besides, the owner would stop paying him if he didn't show up. So, was Fred still managing during this fantastic year?

Let's look at good old Merriam Webster's Dictionary:

man·age

verb

: to have control of (something, such as a business, department, sports team, etc.)

: to take care of and make decisions about (someone's time, money, etc.)

: to direct the professional career of (someone, such as an entertainer or athlete)

Well, Fred had control of a "department;" the kitchen. He made decisions about staff work hours, wages and bonuses. Did he "direct their professional careers?" Kind of. He directed them away from kitchens if they couldn't live up to the restaurant's standards. Occasionally he had the opportunity to tell an outstanding employee when it was time to move on to bigger and better things. So yes, he managed. What Fred didn't seem to have time for was to work individually with each staff member to help them (and the restaurant) climb to the next level. Either the kitchen staff had the talent to succeed, or they only had enough talent or ambition to be adequate and maintain. Fred would have preferred to work with people who exceled rather than accepted just being adequate, but realistically the salaries at this restaurant were only geared to adequacy.

Are you hearing what we're hearing in this example? Yes, Fred was essentially a manager, but he was only "adequate" himself. He didn't really try to move staff beyond their current level and certainly not push himself either. If he had the skill to distinguish between personal attitudes and talents within his staff, why did he limit himself? Why didn't he look for an opportunity to either fantastically develop talent, or to work with highly talented people daily at another place?

One potential problem for Fred was the "lull of management." He put in his years, paid his dues, and made it to management. But his own supervisor didn't challenge him, and he was satisfied with the salary and few perks that went along with being a manager. Overall, his "manager" mindset caused him to miss out on making his job more interesting for himself and his staff.

The good news is that a shifting of gears could transform this manager and all others like him.

So what's *right* about managing?   Most books that encourage a new way of thinking tell you all of the bad things about managing while extolling the benefits of leading instead. But there are some tasks which a manager's mentality is what's called for. One big area that requires a management mindset is dealing with the day-to-day administrivia. We have all dealt with it – the lists that show person X was 28 minutes short of a full work week, while person Y put in 52 minutes beyond a full week and now wants a little time off. It's the filing of last week's work assignments in a folder that may or may not be looked at ever again. In Fred's case it's making sure there's enough soap for the dishwasher, and checking the date of the next expected soap delivery. It's all the details that a manager has to pay attention to so that his or her own supervisor has nothing to grouse about.

The good manager must also be able to "manage up." This includes being able to convince those above him to allow changes to the menu or physical changes to the kitchen; to allow the purchase of products from different vendors; to bring ideas to the large corporation that owns fifty identical restaurants in a dozen states. Sure, not all managers are allowed to interact with high-level leaders, but they need to have the communication skills to do so if they ever hope to move higher.

Bottom line: Fred is an excellent manager if the company only wants someone to maintain the status quo. But Fred is an unlikely candidate for promotion if the company has a vision to excel.

What's wrong with "typical" managing?

"The truth is that many people set rules to keep from making decisions."
– Mike Krzyzewski

"Make sure that team members know they are working with you, not for you."
– John Wooden.

When we refer to "typical" managing, we mean the way it's been perceived by workers since the early industrial revolution. The perception that the primary job of a manager is to *issue orders*. For example, "Next quarter we expect a 10% increase in production, and by the way, as of today we're eliminating overtime," which simply translates to "You all better produce more right now or there'll be hell to pay." Then there's the related perception of managers losing touch with the "real" jobs the workers are doing, as in, "She doesn't get out of her office more than an hour a week, she has no idea what it takes to do my job." And there's the perception of managers playing politics, looking for better jobs for themselves while ignoring their workers' development or growth.

But coaching is just the opposite.

"I've never felt my job was to win basketball games – rather, that the essence of my job as a coach was to do everything I could to give my players the background necessary to succeed in life."
– Bobby Knight.

Coaching as an alternative

In 1950, UCLA Bruins football coach "Red" Sanders said to his team,

---

"Men, I'll be honest. Winning isn't everything. Men, it's the only thing!"

Packers coach Vince Lombardi is on record as using the phrase in 1959. No matter who you credit, it's seems like such a clever phrase! Indeed, winning is the whole point of playing isn't it? Dominate and crush all competitors – what could be more worthwhile? Oh, don't trouble yourself that the not-so-hidden meaning behind that phrase is "do whatever it takes to win, the end justifies the means." In other words, hang ethics, scrap laws - either win or die trying.

While it sometimes seems as though the American business landscape has drifted into such murky realms, no one should lose sight of the fact that, while football may be big business, *business is not football.* There is no single top trophy. Instead there are hundreds of thousands of businesses that employ people and offer products and services. Some interact as competitors one month and collaborators the next. Sure, there are losers, those businesses that fail. And there are businesses that make tons of money, businesses that make little profit but are the best in their niche, non-profits that excel and non-profits that disappear when their causes (or supporters) dry up. And every iteration in between.

Businesses need to succeed, but there are more definitions of success than can be found on the playing field of any particular sport. Nonetheless, coaching (the "managing" of teams) has a great deal to offer and teach the business world. Our goal is to show how changing the mindset from "manage" to "coach" can invigorate everyone from a single worker to a department, or an entire organization.

Let's look again at Merriam Webster's Dictionary:

coach

verb

: to teach and train (an athlete or performer)

: to teach, train, and direct (a sports team)

: to teach (a student) privately rather than in a class

So the two verbs, manage and coach, appear to have somewhat similar definitions, but they are very different. The *behaviors* of a manager are immensely different from the behaviors of a coach. Both socially and culturally the two are perceived in different lights. "Managing" looks like pushing people around while "coaching" looks like a teacher on a mission to elevate every student.

Here's John Calipari's definition of his role as coach:

- Nurturer
- Protector
- Challenger
- Teacher
- Promoter
- A Father

Let's dig deeper. Rarely does a coach have the opportunity to literally create from scratch a brand new team where none existed before. Usually a coach steps into an open position with an existing team and an existing "playbook" of standard operating procedures. So the first thing a coach must do is understand and analyze everything related to that existing team. Who are the members, how does each perform as an individual, how effective are those individuals as a team? What's the condition of the team mentally, physically and emotionally? The team's equipment? The team's facilities? What has been the Standard Operating Procedures (SOP) and for how many years have they been in place? What resources (besides the team members) are available to the coach? Who does this team normally compete against, and what are those competitors' strengths and weaknesses? Who are the "customers" for what the team produces? Are those customers strong supporters, moderate supporters, challenging supporters, or an angry mob? What are the goals and objectives of the existing coaching staff? How effective has the existing staff been in the recent past, and if the new coach has to release under-performing staff, does he have the resources to hire the quality staff he'd like? So many questions, so much to learn so quickly! Is it any wonder the first year for a new coach is considered a re-building year? And yet that new coach is expected to show early successes. At a minimum, the team is expected to show improvement over the previous year.

So how does the new coach succeed? One personal encounter at a time, one practice session at a time!

"My credo is "Players First." It drives everything I do as a coach. Notice that it's plural, not singular."
– John Calipari

Calipari talks about Robert Greenleaf's "Servant Leadership" and how it was a positive influence on his life (and coaching). Calipari explains it this way, "The underpinning of his philosophy could not be simpler: Institutions serve people, not the other way around." And "I measure my success by the success of those whom I'm serving."

"The best test, and difficult to administer, is: Do those served grow as persons?"
– Robert K. Greenleaf

Coach!

Coaching as a means to excel

Common Goals

---

*"Gettin' good players is easy. Gettin' 'em
to play together is the hard part."*
– Casey Stengel

*"On this team, we're all united in a
common goal: to keep my job."*
– Lou Holtz

Most teams succeed in part because they have and know what their common goals are. Having common goals allows everyone on the team to know why the team exists and it makes it possible for each team member to make role-based decisions. It's why an overarching vision is so valuable. A vision is *the* goal. It's the top level goal for the organization. A common, top-level goal provides direction and purpose. A shared direction and purpose.

Calipari expounded on the need for a driving vision, a purpose. "I ask the young men…"What is your 'why?'" Why are you playing basketball for the University of Kentucky, and what do you hope to achieve?" Easily applicable to any organization. Why are you working for your company? What do you hope to achieve? Although your first thought might be to say, I'm working here to make a living…that doesn't really explain your "why." Why that company? Why are you doing that job? If the only reasons you can identify are the paycheck then you will come to regret your choices.

Another commonality a team (and the coach) leans on are values. Values define a ruleset for behavior. If the team's vision, goals, and values are shared, every team member can make the proper call when necessary.

In business there is no March Madness or Super Bowl hysteria, no trophies or post-game interviews. In business there are only satisfied or dissatisfied workers, satisfied or dissatisfied customers, satisfied or dissatisfied shareholders. Winning does not require crushing some opposing organization. Instead, winning means being successful year after year, and during all that time, having everyone on the team fully aware of and engaged in supporting the common goals.

Leadership generally *assumes* everyone knows the common goals while having no real assurance or confidence that the managers and workers share (or are even aware) of the goals. Compare that to a coach. If the coach has a coaching staff, common goals are expressed and re-expressed continuously. Every team member knows and supports those common goals. If anything, some team members might feel like they are reminded of vision, goals and values *too* often. But the repetition works on many levels, leaving no doubts as to where the coach stands, and thus enabling team members to make all kinds of long range, short range, and immediate tactical decisions. This enables their standard operating procedures (SOPs) to be revised on the fly to match any current situation. "Improvisation" actually comes into play when team members see immediate-but-brief opportunities. And innovation is possible because everyone is working from the same playbook.

It's a frequently used tool for creating teamwork - finding a common enemy. Old combatants become allies when there is a common enemy for them to overcome. World War II found those who normally were at each other's throats fighting as allies against the axis powers. And the Axis powers joined forces (against expectations) because of a common goal (and in at least one case – serious coercion).

In "Independence Day," Roland Emmerich's 1996 fun ride, a common enemy brought all the nations of the Earth together and a common goal; survival.

Granted, these are extreme cases, but the theory holds in even the most mundane scenarios. In pro sports we see the power of common goals to bring a team together. Teams with less talent but better focus on a common goal have won games they weren't supposed to. The best coaches start (and end) every season by clearly defining the goals for the team. Then they define goals for each player. Goals provide direction and focus.

Goals are critical to individual success – common goals are critical to team success.

Let's look at the smallest team size possible – a team of two. Imagine if the Bryan brothers (of US professional tennis fame) didn't have the same goals? They would have a hard time achieving success. How about a marriage? If the spouses don't have common goals it not only makes it difficult for either of them to be successful, but that lack of a common purpose can actually tear them apart. Let's say one of the two wants to achieve a certain financial status (millionaire for example) but the other wants to have a large family. To achieve the first goal both spouses may want to work full time (with a decent amount of overtime sprinkled in) and invest their money wisely. They'll want to live as cheaply as possible early in the marriage so they can build up their wealth. But, for the second goal they may need to start the family early (so they have time to have enough children) and therefore they cannot both work as much as they need to become millionaires.

Yes, you may be able to devise a plan where both goals can work together...but what if the two individuals don't share these goals. What if one feels driven to be a millionaire and the other only lukewarm? What if only one of the two wants a big family? Imagine the stress put on the marriage. This is a scenario with only two team members. Expand the scenario to an organization or team with ten employees. Or fifty. How about a three hundred and fifty person organization?

We've worked with numerous organizations of varying size and every one of them benefited from clearly articulated goals. The first step to having a common goal is to define, develop, and share the goals of the organization. The easiest way to ensure common goals is for the leader of the organization to set a large, overarching goal which provides direction for the entire organization. In the organizations we've helped, they all had problems when the goals were not understood or shared by all. This plays out with boards of directors, leadership teams, or work units. If the marketing team can't see how their unit goals mesh with those of your design team, and the design team can't see how their goals work with the goals of the production units – your organization is at enormous risk of working against each other rather than with each other.

So, while common goals help pull your teams together, without them the organization is a set of disparate units actually working against each other's intent, not unlike a sports team running willy-nilly across a field wondering why it can't score points.

Common goals help mitigate the existence of silos. For any organization to succeed you need to foster an attitude of "us and a bigger us" rather than an "us and them" viewpoint.

By clearly articulating the purpose for the team's existence (mission) and the goals (including a vision if applicable) of the team – everyone can make good decisions when necessary. Rather than paralyze the team by making it hard (or impossible) for the front line workers to make decisions – if the team understands the direction they are moving in and what they are trying to achieve, everyone can make wise decisions. What happens if you get a call from the front office asking for a change in priority? What if the customer requests a modification to the delivery schedule? What if there is an emergency stoppage or supply shortage? How do the front line workers make a call? Or do they all just come to a standstill on the field while status reports matriculate upstairs to management?

But isn't that what managers do – make the tough decisions? Yes, but how many of today's business managers are as engaged in their team's play as a coach is? Even a coach can only call a few time-outs to re-assess a situation. And no coach can see the playing field from each team member's perspective. You have to develop the ability of every player to make decisions based on the current situation. This is why you practice. But being able to execute; the results of practice, isn't enough. You have to know the right play to call at the right time – and that requires a full understanding of the team's goals.

Every coach dreams of having players who are in tune with their values, plans, and goals. Such players are called "coaches on the field, court, or diamond." The idea isn't that the coach has all the power and only she can wield it, but that the coach can count on one or more of the team members to instantly take on that role when a sudden threat or opportunity arises.

Caring

"I'd say handling people is the most important thing you can do as a coach. I've found every time I've gotten into trouble with a player, it's because I wasn't talking to him enough."
– Lou Holtz.

A beautiful aspect of coaching over managing is the concern the coach has for each and every player. It is very clear to all involved that the better the player, the better the team. All organizations want their teams (units) to be successful, but in sports you also want each player to reach or better yet, exceed their potential.

In business, we don't normally see this concern with the individual like we do in sports. In business, leadership is focused on the team's results, not necessarily the individual's capability, skills, or talent. In sports it's just the opposite.

The coach knows that while the team focuses on the common goal, one of the best ways to achieve those goals is to help each player on the team excel. In the book The Professional Development Toolbox (by Martin Klubeck), he discusses one of the starkest differences between business and sports, managers and coaches. In business we find that managers actually hesitate to develop their workforce. Rather than grow their staff, they only want to do as much as necessary to keep them up-to-speed with their job descriptions. This is a fascinating attitude. You might wonder why a manager would refrain from developing his staff. Two reasons tell it all.

Reason One – fear of losing their employees to other companies (possibly competitors). Reason Two – fear of being replaced in their *own* job by the newest star. Both reasons come down to the same thing – "managers" don't want their staff to be successful. Oh, they'd be happy for the team and the organization to be successful, but not the individual.

Managers work hard to build what they think is a well-oiled machine. They think they've created a productive and efficient team which gets the job done and in turn makes the manager look good. They see little benefit from individual success, actually they see mostly risk. If workers are highly trained and highly successful in their field they'll get noticed by head hunters and the organization's competition. Best case? The manager has to offer her more salary. Worst case? The worker will take one of the offers coming her way and leave the manager shorthanded.

Why in the world would a manager spend time and money to help a worker change jobs or companies?

This may be the single largest difference between a coach and a manager.

At every level, coaches don't expect their players to leave when they get better - they KNOW they will leave. In high school, they graduate after four years and go to college on an athletic scholarship (if they are good enough). At the college level, they can move on anywhere from 1 year into the program up to their last year of eligibility. It could be to turn pro (the minority) or to pursue the rest of their life. At the professional level players are traded, follow free agency, or retire early due to injury. At all levels coaches know they will have their players for only a short period of time, especially short in comparison to what businesses look for.

It used to be that workers spent their entire careers with a single company. In pro sports this is a rare occurrence, and it's becoming even less likely in college sports where players transfer if they believe it would better their chances for playing time or prospects for making the "big show." The move of LeBron James – Cleveland's franchise and marquee player to Miami was a great example. And his move back to Cleveland after four years in Florida is another. Even life-long icons like Brett Favre, Paul Pierce and Peyton Manning changed teams.

But it doesn't matter. Coaches know their job is to develop each player to reach or possibly exceed their potential. Regardless of what the future holds, each coach works hard to help each player be the best they can be.

And this makes sense because the goal of the coach, and the team, is to win. A coach wants to have the most productive, efficient and effective team she can have. Most sports teams have a year or less to prove themselves and be successful. You might think this makes the comparison unfair.

But we don't agree.

"What keeps me going is not winning, but the quest for reaching potential in myself as a coach and my kids as divers. It's the pursuit of excellence."
– Ron O'Brien

Any business has annual success criteria. It may be the profit-margin, sales, or memberships. It may be the number of houses built or the number of graduates. Sports is not the only industry which measures success each year. And like the best teams, good organizations want *sustained* success. It's not enough to win one game. It's not enough to be the conference, division, or state champion. Those are great successes along the way, but teams want national championships and continued success. They want to become a "dynasty."

If you have a common, clearly articulated, set of goals for your team – you can achieve successes each year and build toward sustained excellence. But to be the best you'll need to develop your team members to their fullest potential.

> *"The quality of a person's life is in direct proportion to their commitment to excellence, regardless of their chosen field of endeavor."*
> *– Vince Lombardi*

You want innovative, creative, self-starting, self-disciplined, dedicated workers. While you can't train most of those attributes, you can (and should) develop the skills and abilities of each worker. If you show true concern for the development and success of each and every worker, you'll find that the employees' attitudes will match your needs.

Caring about each person's development and success is much more than a quaint idea. It's an idea critical to the overall "care and feeding" of any team. If the coach only sees players for a few minutes a week, then those players bond with the coaching assistants, and begin to feel out of touch, tend to feel like merely paid help, more or less equivalent to the machines and tools around them.

So, yes, as a Coach instead of a manager, you have to focus a lot of your efforts on helping each individual improve. You want each employee to achieve individual success AND you want the team to also be at its best. Be aware – your desire to have each worker be individually successful has to be sincere; insincerity cannot be disguised and will poison the well.

Perhaps the most useful chapter in Lou Holtz' book, Winning Every Day; The Game Plan for Success (HarperBusiness, 1999) is titled, "Can I Trust You?" This is a basic question every player asks about his coach, teammate, and agent. It's also the question the coach asks of each player. Trust is essential to creating a successful team – in sports and business. Holtz rightly states that "All relationships are based on mutual trust. Without it there is nothing."

Although he was a head football coach, he knows the lessons he learned in coaching sports translated directly to the business world. "If employees and employer doubt each other's integrity, what do you have? An organization where people spend too much time watching their backs and too little time growing their profits."

It's not about you, it's about your players and your team and your organization. "If you hold a position of authority, you also have an obligation to do all you can to create an environment where others can succeed." And this is a head coach speaking – one who has reached the pinnacle of his profession.

The Game Plan

Putting team above self

"There is another side [to ego] that can wreck a team or an organization. That is being distracted by your own importance. It can come from your insecurity in working with others. It can be the need to draw attention to yourself in the public arena. It can be a feeling that others are a threat to your own territory. These are all negative manifestations of ego, and if you are not alert to them, you get diverted and your work becomes diffused. Ego in these cases makes people insensitive to how they work with others and it ends up interfering with the real goal of any group efforts."
– Bill Walsh.

"This isn't an easy task in a society where celebration of ego is the number one national pastime."
– Phil Jackson

Putting team first, above self, is the only way for it to reach it's potential, and when you look at the team's success as the goal, it's also the only way for each worker to be successful.

This concept has been preached to business for many years. It has gone by the name of teamwork, collaboration, and servant leadership. It continues to be offered (under different names) because it has yet to be embraced in corporate America, while sports has accepted it as the best path to success.

Basketball is a great example in this case; more so at the high school and college levels than in the pros. As a player, you can dominate the game. You can take every shot for your team and win scoring titles while watching your team fail to even make it to the playoffs. Coaches see these selfish players for what they are – and work to quickly get them off the team if they can't change their attitudes. If the coach ignores it, their teams consistently fall short at the end of the year. One reason a coach may ignore the issue is that top leadership loses sight of the underlying goals of the organization. Many times the selfish person is also the star player. Excuses abound:

1. The player is your best player
2. The player has no faith or confidence in the team
3. The player has lost sight of the organization's vision
4. Leadership has lost sight of the organization's vision
5. Leadership is too cowardly to get rid of their best individual player even though they know the team may function better without him

Let's look a little deeper at each reason.

The best player

Funny how this happens. Rarely do you see a bench player, what we call a role player, being selfish. The best players get a lot of accolades and recognition. If the team wins, they are the ones getting interviewed. If the team loses they are rarely blamed – because, well, they're the best players on the team! There is the exception where if you are one of the best players in the game, you get criticized if your team loses – there's always something you could have or should have done differently. You should have taken the last shot. You should have passed to the open player instead of taking the last shot. This is the world of Lebron James and Peyton Manning. But they are the exception. On most teams the best players are credited for wins and commiserated with when the team loses. This sets them up to put themselves before the team.

And as with many things in life (leadership being one of them), the person who has the hardest time resisting temptation is the one who can do the most harm if she doesn't succeed. When the best player is selfish it can destroy the chemistry of the team. If you don't think team chemistry is important in your business environment you haven't been paying attention. You cannot afford selfish players – no matter how good they are.

The player has no faith or confidence in the team

Sometimes this is the underlying cause for the selfishness. When a player believes the team is incapable of achieving its goals, the player has two choices – give up on the team (and only look out for self) or step up as a leader and try to make the team better. It takes a special type of person to *step up* to the challenge rather than *step on* others. So, it falls back to the coach to mentor the player – especially the best ones – to help them take on this role. The simplest and most important first step is to stop rewarding the selfish players for their individual successes. You have to demand leadership from your best, you have to expect them to help the team be better. You have to coach them on how to help make others better. And to do these things you can't reward the selfish behavior.

This is hard. Very hard. You have to actually *know* your team, know your players, and pay attention to the interactions between them. Most business managers don't take the time to do any of this. All they do is look at the performance measures and reward accordingly. It's too much effort to do more. The manager gives out work and then provides recognition based on the results. The manager misses or ignores the teamwork, chemistry, and overall success of the team.

We used the term "manager" throughout on purpose – because coaches know better. In business, managers expect the staff to let them know if a coworker isn't being a "team player." In other words, managers expect the workers to do their job for them. Besides simply being wrong, more often than not, it doesn't work. The role players won't "rat out" the best and brightest for a couple of reasons. First – it's not a "team" attitude. Secondly, since the manager keeps rewarding the selfish worker, who wants to tell the manager that she is wrong? Who wants to be the one to tell the manager that the person she's been recognizing for strong performance is a non-team player? The one who is most likely to complain is the superstar! This selfish worker will not hesitate to blame any small or large failures on everyone else – and why not? His productivity clearly shows through the performance measures that it isn't his fault.

The selfish player has lost sight of the organization's vision

Even if your top player has faith in the team, he also has to keep focused on the top level goals. Without this focus he can easily fall into the habit of only trying to succeed at his small part of the puzzle. In sports we see this in the player who does their job – and nothing more. No cheering for his teammates. No extra hustle. No intangibles like congratulating teammates when they do well or showing empathy when they don't. If any team member forgets the things the organization is trying to achieve it's easy to stop putting the organization first.

Leadership has lost sight of the vision

Based on everything we've shared so far, this may now be obvious: If leadership loses sight of the organization's top goals, the team will notice. Leadership will reward the wrong things, focus on the wrong indicators of success, and recognize the wrong people. Leadership has to not only stay focused on the bigger picture, but it must also help the rest of the organization stay focused. Along with this focus, leadership has to always remember that team success comes first. Of course, leaders can fall into the same selfish traps your best workers can. Your shining stars who ascend to leadership positions quickly can suffer the same problems as your top player. Rather than focusing on the team's success, they can easily get wrapped up in personal achievements. If you have a selfish leader, you're in even more trouble than having a selfish player. The selfish leader not only keeps the team from reaching its potential, but he is also the worst manager possible.

The simplest way to look at it is; "selfishness kills." It kills an organization from the inside. This is true of sports teams or businesses.

Leadership is too cowardly to get rid of a selfish player

Another problem which comes from the top is when leadership, in spite of realizing that it has a selfish player, is too cowardly to discipline or get rid of the player. Of course, it would be best to help that player change. But if that's not possible, leadership has to take the tough stance and kick that player off the team. This can be done through a trade, buying out her contract, or by kicking her off the team. Many times we don't want to abandon a superstar who has helped the team...but in truth, the selfish star has only been helping herself.

The bottom line is leadership has to make the tough calls…it's why they get paid the big bucks. And that tough call is dictated by what the team needs to function properly. It may require removing one of your best. It may require changing processes that have been in place for years. It may require changing the direction of the organization.

Remember the irony – if your best player is selfish, he will tear your organization apart. Your best player may be the worst person for your team.

The selfish superstar is like a sales rep who oversells the capacity of the company's production department – he collects monthly bonuses while production goes crazy putting in overtime that eats up the profits. You can have workers who selfishly only look at their own reputation, rewards and recognition. Many times this shows up as information or knowledge hording. Or in workers who are only concerned with their own workloads and productivity. They don't work on teams well, they don't help others, and they only do what gets them recognition.

Leveraging strengths

"Selecting the right person for the right job is the largest part of coaching."
– Phil Crosby.

"The most important message I have to communicate to players is that each of them has a role, and that role is based upon what each player does well."
– Muffet McGraw

There has been an admirable movement lately toward focusing on strengths instead of weaknesses. Tom Rath's strengthsfinder.com is a great place to start if you want to learn about your individual strengths. The idea is to find your personality strengths and to build on those instead of trying to become something you're not. Rather than spend your time and energy trying to become better at the things you can't (and arguably never will) do well, you should focus on your strengths and become exceptional. You can best help yourself and your team by becoming the best version of you, you can be.

It doesn't make sense for a talented running back to work on kicking field goals instead of improving his ability to read a block. That's a pretty easy one right? The same as you wouldn't expect a programmer to focus her energies on her ability to write a humorous blog post. But the question is how far do you take this?

The days of the Renaissance Man are pretty much behind us. In every sport (and job) there are now distinct levels of specialization. A running back needs to work on his skillset for being a better runner. Within the skills needed, he will have strengths (like reading blocks, accelerating through a gap) and weaknesses (like fumbling or blocking a blitzing defender). Obviously, for him to excel in his position, he has to improve on the weaknesses – otherwise he won't get to play. But his "weakness" has to be at least within the *realm* of his strengths. Based on his complete set of skills, strengths and his passion, he becomes a running back. Not a kicker or quarterback. He isn't focusing on golf, tennis, or nuclear science. He's focusing on his strengths and his passion around those strengths.

As a coach it is imperative that you find out the strengths of your players so you can help them develop and the team can leverage those strengths to excel. Within those skills and roles in which they excel, you will help each player improve on her particular strengths while mitigating or eliminating her weaknesses. Sometimes this means changing a person's position. Instead of playing defense you may switch that player to an offensive role. Instead of being a point guard, you may move her to be a shooting guard.

The same has to happen in a business setting. You have to be willing to move your workers into positions which best suit their talents. Instead of being a programmer you may move him to a quality assurance role. Instead of providing second level support the worker may be better suited as a business analyst. It's frightening how often we encounter people who were hired to fill a particular position, and forever-after treated by management as if that position is their destiny. Unlike sports, businesses generally fail to break down job descriptions into specific tasks; if they would do so, they'd discover a treasure trove of untapped skills across the organization – skills being underutilized because the "label" of a current position creates tunnel vision among managers.

One of the truly fun aspects of the corporate environment is realizing the strengths of your players, especially since those strengths aren't as readily apparent as someone who can hit a three-pointer 45% of the time.

Leveraging strengths is one of the most obvious ways managers can benefit by switching to coaching. Managers need to find out where each person's passion lies, where their strengths are, and how those two factors can work within the business model in which the organization functions. Helping a worker find his niche is extremely rewarding. Like a coach who helps an athlete find the right sport and then within the sport, the right position, you can do the same for any worker.

Based on the passion and strengths of your worker you should do your best to help her find the right fit. Even if that means a different position, team, unit, or even industry. What if you find that the worker really should be in a totally different career field? You could fire her of course. Or you could be a good coach and help her transition to her proper vocation. What a terrific gift you could give your worker; to help him find his calling in life, to move into a job that makes him happy to come to work every day. The problem is that many managers concentrate only on the work output and forget the concept of worker happiness. Every worker wants to be successful, and generally people feel successful when they are using their talents and skills every day. Ignoring the comfort level of the worker and her self-esteem, is a recipe for mediocrity at best. *And* a regular turnover rate. It's a simple and readily accepted concept – if you love your work, you'll be more productive. And if you feel like you contribute, that your efforts make a difference to the success of the organization – you will be happier in your work.

You can best facilitate that happiness by helping each worker leverage their strengths and concentrate most of their energies on what they do best.

But how about the person who doesn't fit the role and that role is a leadership position? How about a new manager you promoted a year ago who really isn't meant to be in charge? How about a supervisor whose strengths and passion dictates that you move her back into a non-leadership role? How many leaders would be willing to admit the "mistake" and "demote" the worker into a position she will be better suited for, and actually happier in? We tell ourselves that we hesitate because the worker (currently supervisor or manager) would be devastated if we demote her – but in reality, she'd be much happier. It's our own pride that keeps us from admitting that we didn't fully take into account her strengths and weaknesses when we promoted her in the first place.

It's hard, but it's a step that a good coach takes. If the coach selected a player to be the starting quarterback and after a few games realizes that this is not the player's best role, rather than force a square peg into a round hole the coach admits the error and moves the player to a position that better fits his set of skills. You will see quarterbacks become wide receivers or even running backs. You will see wide receivers become defensive corner backs. We can and should do the same in business.

Reviewing "the video"

"I thought we battled and competed against Tennessee. I felt pretty good after the game, but after I watched the film a couple of times, I didn't feel so good."
– Muffet McGraw

One of the great tools coaches use to develop players is reviewing video of practices and competitions. While the coach may look at the video with other coaches to see how the team is doing and how to improve, another major benefit is realized when the coach reviews the video with the player. The coach might review the entire game with the player, identifying what he did right or wrong in unison with the team, or only review specific plays and situations. The good coach not only provides visible and teachable feedback, but trains the player to analyze the film on his own. And what a great tool to have! You can watch any number of replays of the player's performance on a large screen. You can rewind, watch it in slow-motion, or freeze critical frames within plays.

Video allows the player to see himself in relation to the rest of the team, the system, and the process he should be following.

How can you study video in the workplace? We don't have video crews taping our efforts at our desks, on the assembly line, or in the conference room. Although it might be awesome if we did, then again it might just be creepy.

The idea is to provide accurate and honest feedback.

For the corporate world we have to find a substitute for reviewing video, but it has to be far more than simply reviewing the final score. Many managers make the mistake of evaluating performance solely based on the results. But that doesn't provide feedback on the *process*. Too many managers take the easy (and lazy) way out and only evaluate performance based on the end results. This might sound logical but it's broken thinking – what coach waits until the end of the season to evaluate player performance? What coach spends hours talking about the final score or naming the top achievers but fails to spend even a day analyzing player strengths and weaknesses? This strange corporate mentality only works if all you care about are the results and not how they are achieved. To provide useful feedback ("useful" meaning developmental) a coach has to consider how *well* the process was performed or how well the play was executed – not just the results.

Your review has to involve reviewing all the steps taken, the pitfalls found and how the player stumbled, the improvements that must be made, and how the player can practice and perfect those improvements. It requires communication with the worker and teaching her how to review her *own* performance. This is where we will make a pitch for having repeatable processes. If your organization (at whatever level you're at) has repeatable and documented processes that are followed to perform the work – it will make "reviewing the video" much easier. If each worker does her own thing, her own way, it's nearly impossible to review or learn from. By having repeatable processes, each employee can "relive" their performance and identify the same things you would by watching a video:

1. What did she do well?
2. What worked for her? (sometimes it's the process, or part of the process that needs to be addressed, not the player)

3. What didn't work for her?
4. When and why did she circumvent or avoid the process?
5. Considering all these factors, where must improvement occur? And once identified, what resources are available so the player can practice?

As coach, we always want to improve three things:

1. The performance of the individual within the team
2. The overall team performance
3. The process itself

Coaches have to tailor their systems to their talent – at least until they can develop the players they have or recruit the talent they want. We have to do the same. Just because a process is repeatable and documented, that doesn't mean it's perfect. Even if it's a "best practice" – it has to be a fit for the talent *and* skills of your current team.

Just as a sports coach implements a system, businesses implement processes. Just as a sports coach wants to improve those systems so they are the most productive and efficient, we want to do the same with our processes.

Be creative and look for opportunities to "video" your team in action. To paraphrase Yogi Berra, "You can observe a lot by just watching." Are they gathering requirements? Interactions with customers can be recorded; you've surely heard the announcement before the customer service rep picks up the phone: "this call may be recorded for quality purposes". You can video workers doing assembly work, design work, even something as mundane as typing. The key though is to review the tape (or equivalent) with the worker. It's not a tool to judge, it's a tool to provide *feedback* so the worker can improve. Feedback is the key and managers who fail to provide regular and frequent feedback are failing to develop their workers.   With a non-judgmental frame-of-mind, most workers will be glad to "review the video."

Giving credit to the players not the coach

A lion never roars after a kill
– Dean Smith

"If anything goes bad, I did it, if anything
goes semi-good, then we did it, if anything
goes real good, then [the team] did it."
– Coach Bear Bryant

The best coaches do this without thinking. They know that as coach they have a *lot* to do with the success or failure of the team, but the best way to be successful is to spread the credit among the players. In sports – the "player coach" is a rare thing today, but depending on the level, this is not so uncommon in the corporate world. Front line supervisors are sometimes more "doer" than leader. As you climb up the ladder of responsibility you find this much less. You would never expect to find a CEO who is a doer in terms of production or service delivery. But down to the level of special teams coach or any assistant coach, you won't find a sports coach who is also a player. It doesn't matter if you're talking about the pros, college, high school, or club ball...player coaches don't happen much anymore. And this is a very good thing. It's something corporate needs to emulate.

Managers and even supervisors, need to remove themselves from "doing." It may be the hardest thing for a new supervisor to do – especially when that person is promoted from within. The reason you shouldn't try to be both – a doer and a leader, is simple. Being a doer when you are in a position of leadership doesn't help the team succeed.

Most times it makes the workers feel that the manager doesn't have faith in their abilities to get the job done. Even when the help is specifically and explicitly requested by the worker, it can undermine the worker's confidence and position. It sets up a bad precedent. It would never happen in sports – and for good reason. A player can't turn to the coach from the field and say, "Could you come in for me? Just for one play?" Players have to play, coaches coach.   Workers have to do the work, supervisors need to supervise.

This anomaly only occurs in business. Leaders actually applaud a supervisor or manager who rolls up her sleeves and pitches in when needed. We tell managers that they shouldn't ask anything of their team they wouldn't do themselves. But, that doesn't mean they're supposed to do it! Of course in a small operation, you may have to be a doer because you *are* one of the workers. You just happen to also be the owner. But outside of those examples...if you're in a medium to large size organization and you have the title of manager, there are other ways for you to help. There are ways for you to show your support of those who have to work extra hours. Feel free to come in when your team works an overnighter – stay there with them. But stay out of their way. Ask what they need, provide support and supplies. Even buy them pizza if you like. But stay out of their way unless they come to you for decisions only you are authorized to make.

And if you feel you have to chip in on the front line, if you feel you have to get your hands dirty...put on the hat of the temp-worker, not the expert. And definitely not the boss. If you feel you have to show that you're one of the team by working on the line, then make sure you're at the lowest point of the line, take orders from the senior workers, and do it the way *they* do, the way *they* have to. Just realize, if you do this periodically, do it as a show of support rather than part of your normal responsibilities. If you do it in a crisis, everyone will understand the abnormality of the situation but it would still be better if you didn't get on the field. A coach will get their hands "dirty" during practice, training the players and helping them to become better. But when it comes time to play the game, coaches have to stay on the side line. Even if there is an "emergency." Even if the star player is injured, the coach doesn't suit up and get on the field.

Workers have to write the code, clean the floor, and assemble the brakes. Workers have to get the job done. But in business, most of the rewards for team performance seem to go to the managers, who accept the accolades, promotions, and bonuses. It's said that a good manager will share some of that wealth downhill, rewarding her team for helping her reap success.

How bass ackwards can we be? Imagine a coach of any team taking credit for the team's success and then "sharing" some of those accolades downhill. There would be a mutiny in short order. Even the most successful Hall of Fame bound coaches know to give their players the credit when the team succeeds. Listen to Urban Meyer (head coach of Ohio State's 2015 champion football team) talk about the success of his team. Listen to him after his Florida football team won two championships. Listen to him talk about any of his teams which never won less than 8 games in a season…any of his teams! It isn't about him – it's about his players. Everyone, and I mean everyone, knows it has a *lot* to do with him as the head coach. He wins wherever he goes. He is sought after by every program that wants to win a championship. The same was true for John Wooden, then Phil Jackson. Good coaches don't need to take the credit for the team's success – great coaches wouldn't think of it. Dean Smith will always be remembered at North Carolina for *always* embracing and crediting the team.

It's ok to cut down the nets with the team. It's ok to get a Gatorade bath from the team. It's ok to have talk shows, awards, and praise heaped on you as the coach.   But, when asked how YOU did it, how YOU brought home the championship, the easy and correct answer is – YOU didn't. The team did. The same has to be true for the project team or the work unit, or if you're the CEO, for the entire organization.

Taking the blame

---

*"Admit to and make yourself accountable
for mistakes. How can you improve if
you're never wrong?"*
– Pat Summitt

*If you do what we ask you to do, the
victories will belong to you, and the losses
to me*
– Dean Smith

So, this is really unfair. You have to give the credit for any and all successes to your team, but when it comes to failures, you have to take the blame. No credit and all the blame. When the team fails, it's not OK to blame the star player. It's not OK to blame the last player on the bench. When asked "who was to blame for the team failing" there is only one valid answer – the coach.

Why?

One reason is the coach is ultimately responsible for the team's success or failure. It's the coach's system (or processes). It was the coach's responsibility to develop the individual players. It was the coach's responsibility to deal with the personalities, to get the right people on the team; through hires and trades. It was the coach's job to get the wrong people off the team; through firing or trading. The coach has to make the tough calls. The coach has to help the players excel – and reach (if not exceed) their potential. The bottom line is pretty simple…the leader has to take the final blame for the failure. The Samurai understood this, as did the best military leaders.

Sucks eh?

But that's part of being a leader. There *are* ex-coaches who have blamed players for failures. That's why they are "ex" coaches. It erodes the team's faith in the coach. It destroys any chance at loyalty. And, it's wrong. It really is the coach's fault.

It's not a new concept. But, for some reason the corporate world hasn't figured it out fully.

One of the reasons the manager doesn't willingly take the blame for the unit's failures is that she doesn't feel like it's her fault. She feels that most of the vital ingredients to success (and therefore also failure) are beyond her control.

1. Picking your players
2. Trading, releasing, benching players who aren't helping the team
3. Being able to assign work to each player as she sees fit
4. Disciplining unacceptable behavior
5. Rewarding strong performers

Basically, some managers feel that they aren't truly in charge. They don't have the budget or the actual authority to lead.

This is a hard argument. If the manager is only seen as some kind of "scheduler" by senior leadership, she could very well be right. She may have no power or authority to change, effect, or reward her people. She may also have no power over the processes. In essence, she's *not* in charge. In this scenario, the manager has a decision to make. Either she chooses to succumb to her situation and be only a figure-head manager or she can choose to lead anyway (of course she could also quit).

You may have expected us to say she could fight for the authority she needs to get the job done. Perhaps you wanted us to say that she should demand the power to hire and fire as she sees fit. She should be given a budget and control over rewards and recognition. She should have the power to evaluate her staff and have those evaluations mean something.

You can definitely fight for these things. But, the funny thing is, if you aren't a leader – even if you gain the authority, you still won't be a good leader. Granted, it would make life easier for anyone in the position, but it won't solve the underlying problem. If you can't lead (or can't coach), then the authority will only enable you to manage.

So, we propose that the solution isn't to demand the authority (or quit) – the solution is to choose to lead anyway.

"Once you learn to quit, it becomes a habit."
– Vince Lombardi.

It's a lot harder – but it'll be required nonetheless if you do get the authority. So, while you request the power you should already have in your position, make sure you're leading the best you can. Part of that is taking the blame for failures. Even if you didn't pick your team or have little authority to force the team to do as you direct, you still have to find a way to get them to follow you. And blaming them for a failure is definitely not the way to create followers.

Even if you can't fire and hire, you can do the essentials to build a productive team. You can find the strengths and weaknesses of your team. You can develop your team (even without a budget). You can develop processes, improve procedures, and empower your team. You can encourage, assist, and guide. You can coach your team. Granted, your team may not be able to win the championship or be the best unit in the industry (or even the organization), but there are countless stories of good leaders and coaches taking on "misfit" teams and being highly successful. Not having official authority just makes the challenge more meaningful.

Realizing you have to let the players "play the game"

"Success is about having the right person, in the right place, at the right time."
– Pat Summitt

Earlier we wrote that there is little good that comes out of trying to be both a player and a coach. That was an understatement. Actually there is no good that comes from trying to be a player and a coach. The best basketball player in the world, Michael Jordan, failed miserably at it. He was a great player. He may have become a great coach. But even he couldn't do both at the same time.

Even if a good player becomes a good coach (and there are many, such as Doc Rivers or Steve Kerr) – once that player becomes a coach he stops being a player. Professional and amateur sports are pretty smart when it comes to this. Most players have a down period between retiring as a player and trying to become a coach (Jason Kidd being an exception). Most either do sports-casting or assistant coaching for a few years before taking (or being offered) a head coaching job. But in the business world we frequently promote - making a manager of someone - who was a worker the day before!

And who do we pick to be the manager? Usually *our best worker*! Especially when we promote from within, we send a clear message to the new manager. We tell her that she was given the job because of her performance as a worker. And now that we have promoted her, we should want her to take on a different set of responsibilities and a different set of behaviors. The problem is that our mixed message confuses the well-meaning manager. Why wouldn't she try to keep doing what got her the promotion in the first place? Why wouldn't she jump in (and on and over) when a worker is having trouble?

There is a reason most players-who-become-coaches have and need a break between the two roles.

But business takes this one step further (in the wrong direction) and promotes that worker within the team she actually played on! We don't have space in this book to cover all of the psychological problems that will plague the team's chemistry and the manager's authority when that happens. Leave it simply that there's more than one reason a player who becomes a coach doesn't do it for the team he's currently playing for.

As a manager, you have to let the worker do the job. You can't be successful (in the long run) by micro-managing or by doing the work yourself. If your workers can't do the job, you are in *big* trouble. Imagine the worker who successfully covered for his colleagues and did most (if not all) of the hard jobs. And then leadership makes the common mistake of promoting this superhero into the manager's role.

Of course our superhero will continue doing all of the hard tasks and working himself to death. Our superhero won't even be able to change because not only is the work his comfort zone, but he has "trained" all of his workforce (when he was their peer) to bring him the tough stuff. Why would either change?

And when it comes time to hire a replacement for his vacated position on the team or new people through natural attrition? The manager won't want to hire another expert equal to himself because it would undermine his self-worth. So what chance is there that he would hire someone *better* than himself? No, the team is relegated to the replacement of mediocrity with more mediocrity.

But let's look at the scenario if leadership *hadn't* created a player-coach. Suppose that same "expert" was thought to be coach material, and was hired to coach a different team in a different discipline. Then the manager of his former team would be in trouble because the expertise just left. That manager would have to hire better to replace the lost expertise. Or perhaps that manager would have to do the harder job of developing the employees left behind. Most times the other employees have the capability, but over time have lost the accountability or desire to improve. Is this team a little worse-for-the-wear for a couple months? Possibly. But the team and the new manager also received a wake-up call – peak performance is a *team* obligation, not the duty of a single expert or star player.

And the expert who was promoted? If he is put in as a manager in a new discipline area will he shine? Who knows? If leadership chose the worker based solely on previous expertise, that expertise may not translate to coaching others. If leadership chose the worker because, *besides* being an expert, he displayed a number of management and leadership traits, then he may be ready to study coaching in earnest and put that new learning to the test.

Some of the best coaches were never great players. Coaching is *not* the same as being a player; great, good, or a role player. Managing is not the same as being a good or great worker. The jobs are different.

And good coaches know this. Good coaches, even if they were great players, know that they have to develop a new set of skills. They have to take all of the strengths of good coaches they've observed in their careers and try to emulate them. They need to avoid the mistakes, pitfalls, and weaknesses they've witnessed from coaches they've had in the past.

Ever notice that the sports superstars usually aren't the ones who become coaches? It's usually the role player, the gym rat. The one who loved the game and learned and learned and learned. This of course could be because the superstar made more than enough money to never need to work again...but it can also be that the superstar didn't have the right temperament to coach or the right skill set. Again Jason Kidd could be an exception – but look at most of the players who became coaches. Some have a chance at the Hall of Fame as a coach but nearly none made it as a player. And very few Hall-of-Fame players have a chance to attain equal recognition as a coach.

And they in no way imagine that they will still play the game. Even if they think they can do the job better than one of their players, they can't take their place. Even if a manager thinks she can do the task better, it's no longer her job. As a manager her job is to coach and lead...not do.

"Seek out quality people, acknowledge their talents, and let them do their jobs."
– Pat Summitt

Maintaining relationships

"A common mistake among those who work in sport is spending a disproportional amount of time on "x's and o's" as compared to time spent learning about people."
— Mike Krzyzewski.

It's all about the relationships. Relationships between coach and player. Between player and coach. Between Head Coach and assistant coaches. Between players. Between coaches from opposing teams. Between the owners and the coach.

Everything comes down to the relationship. Think of it as team chemistry. The coach has to ensure the team functions smoothly and effectively. To do so the team has to work together. Sports are a great model to put up against the corporate world. Can you imagine any effective team that has siloes all over the place? How about players who won't help other players? How about segregation and isolation?

They don't work in sports. We'd rather have a team of mediocre players who have good chemistry and work well together than an all-star team *without* chemistry. First of all the good chemistry team will be a heck of a lot easier to coach. The all-star team with no chemistry will be a constant headache and annoyance. We would hate coming to work. But the good chemistry team would be fun to work with and to coach. The good chemistry team would win more than you think, and when they win, it would be fun and rewarding. When they suffer a loss, it wouldn't be due to lack of effort or bad attitudes. It would be a learning experience which they'd use (with the coach's help) to get better.

Yup, we'd take the good chemistry, hardworking, willing-to-develop team over the all-star team with poor chemistry any day of the week.

So, the coach is responsible for putting together this good chemistry team. Even if the coach is given top-notch talent, his job is to direct that chemistry and make it work like a secret weapon. If the chemistry is weak, it's his job to change it. That might even mean trading away (or firing) the "best" player on the team! It may mean shaking things up drastically. But it's all about the relationships – not just between the coach and the players, but also between the coach and his staff. And a lot of it has to do with the relationships among the players.

These relationships, and resulting chemistry, are perhaps the number one factor in determining how great your team can be. Without positive relationships, work becomes a grind. And when anyone dreads coming to work, the whole team's productivity suffers. Even if you are personally driven to do your best, you won't have either the synergy or innovation necessary to perform as a great team.

Great teams are formed through relationships.

In addition to the coach being responsible for ensuring that his team's chemistry is "cooking," the coach also builds a positive relationship with each player. This is confirmed by most business surveys. The number one factor for employee satisfaction is the relationship with your direct supervisor. Close behind is the relationship the worker has with co-workers. Gallup captured this under the question, "do you have a best friend at work." Imagine what it would be like to play on a team where you didn't get along with anyone. Or where you didn't have a positive, healthy, nurturing relationship with your coach! Imagine working where you aren't happy, where you don't get along with your co-workers, and where your relationship with your boss is more adversarial than supportive. Unfortunately, many people toil in this environment every day.

Poor relationships drag down a team, eroding it from within.

Good relationships build champions.

It's true for sports and it's equally true for business.

A good coach builds strong relationships with his players which last a lifetime. A good coach cares for his people and cares about his people. His relationships with his players is critical to his success, but more importantly it's critical to the player's future success. When UNC coach Dean Smith died at 83, players he'd coached forty years earlier were making public statements about how they *still* think of him at every major decision point in their lives. What an amazing testimonial to the relationships he built with his players!

Just like organizational culture, you can't leave forging positive relationships up to the workers to do on their own and hope for the best. You have to create an environment that encourages positive relationships. Your workers have to feel more than comfortable with building ties with co-workers. Your workers have to feel part of a family, part of a team. The best teams build ties that never end. Even if the player is traded to a competing team, even arch-rivals, they not only keep their personal ties, but maintain high regard for their professional ties.

Since a poor relationship will kill a team, the coach has to pay careful attention to the health of all these relationships. If there are bad seeds on the team, the coach has to weed them out. If there is conflict he has to mediate and moderate. Along with making sure the team plays well and gets the job done, he has to help foster strong bonds.

If your team encounters conflicts, you can't ignore the problem. If you leave this up to the workers, sometimes they'll fix it themselves. But most times you'll end up losing good workers to other companies because they'll decide the headaches aren't worth it. If you don't fix it as the coach, their easiest recourse is to find a new team to play for.

Maintaining relationships isn't just an on-the-job activity. Relationships begin before the players join the team – during the recruiting process – and remain critical to team success day in and day out. When a player eventually leaves your team – to trades, for a better position, or retiring – the relationship remains important. Some people call this networking. But that belittles the essence of it. "Networking" carries a connotation of insincerity – say whatever it takes to make a connection. Networking implies wanting to build contacts – and if you want to be optimistic, these contacts will all be mutually beneficial. You scratch some backs and they reciprocate. In the more cynical view of networking, you use them and split before they can use you back. "Relationship" doesn't have the same meaning or any of those negative connotations. Rather than creating networks, coaches build relationships, and a good manager will learn difference.

> *"I was a demanding coach, but my players knew that I cared for them and that my caring didn't stop when they graduated and went off to their careers"*
> *– Dean Smith*

Practice

---

*"The will to win is meaningless without
the will to prepare!"*
– Joe Gibbs.

Ever notice how some managers spend more time focusing on the time clock than on staff development? Bad managers think their job is about running rough shod over those lazy workers, ensuring the company gets its fair effort for every dollar paid when they should actually be working hard to help each worker reach his or her potential. But instead, they focus on monitoring the worker's time and behavior.

Some managers want to remove the water cooler because workers congregate and gripe – as if removing the venue would stop the dissent.

Some managers think they should just supervise their people instead of coaching them. And if they're willing to admit that they shouldn't "manage" people, they want to at least manage their people's time. The really bad managers don't think work is a place for fun. If they hear employees laughing, they figure their staff aren't working hard enough.

These managers don't understand the concepts of practice, match play, or time to "goof off."

"The key is not the will to win. Everybody has that. It is the will to prepare to win that is important."
– Bobby Knight

Some managers believe that every worker should get everything right the first time and every time. They believe that they should hire people who can fully perform the job at the level wanted. There isn't *time* for a teachable moment. There isn't time for training and development. Employees are always on the clock, always producing.

In the real world this equates to no mistakes, no risk-taking, and definitely no fun.

But a good coach knows that it's all about the practice. In practice we get better. In practice we try new things. In practice we perfect our systems and processes. Practice is the opportunity for the coach to help the player improve – without it costing a game. You can't stop the game to teach the player how to do the job. You have to do that in practice. And the *best* teams (actually all teams) practice. At the end of a long season, even the two best teams in any sport – the last two teams standing, about to find out who THE champion will be, have practices leading up to the final game.

Practice is essential to improvement.

So how does you, as a business coach, hold a practice?

Programmers have used practice and test environments for ages. But there rest of us could also benefit from practice. In business, you can have actual practice sessions where you go through procedures and processes as a team or with an individual. This is especially helpful with emergency procedures.

If you can perform a process, you can *practice* performing it. The how is definitely possible...it's the willingness and understanding of the need that's the tricky part. How many workers or managers would consider "merely" practicing their craft? Usually the only practice time comes when someone is learning how to do the job.

But in sports this isn't the case. In sports, we practice even when we have games every week or every other day. And that makes sense. In sports, we are always trying to perfect our trade, improve our effectiveness and efficiency. We also frequently practice because the coach is implementing new plays. How many new ways are there for someone to cook a burger at a fast-food restaurant? Actually no new ways...as the process is extremely well defined. So, is it worth it to practice so the employee can become even better at making those burgers? Watching Sponge Bob Squarepants ™, I'd have to say yes. Even a fast food crew will benefit from practice.

We *can* treat some of our work in the same way we would a practice. We can work side by side with the employee, and coach them on the process, help them refine their methods and improve their results. It should be obvious this can have significant benefits for the worker, the manager, and the organization.

By providing real practice time or using a work session as a practice session, the manager demonstrates to the worker that his performance is important to the organization. This not only tells the worker that his development is important, it increases his confidence and prepares him to teach others.

OK, maybe you believe in practice. How about match play?

Isn't every day at work (other than training or practice) match play? Isn't that the biggest difference between sports and business? In sports, players only really have to work occasionally – football players only play once a week, but most employees work 9-5, 5 days a week (if not a lot more). This may be true – but all tasks are not created equal. There are routine tasks and critical tasks. Firefighters practice for those occasions when they will be called upon to save lives (including their own). Police have less practice time, but they also tend to have a number of routine tasks – patrolling, traffic stops, traffic control, writing and filing reports, etc. But police also have plenty of critical tasks that require regular practice and testing.

Consider your own job. Do you work equally hard all day long? Or are some tasks more critical? Do you have paperwork, documentation, or administrative tasks? Do you have email to process, equipment to clean? If so, you aren't really in match play mode all the time. Match play could be dealing with crises or putting out fires. It could be intense project work vs. maintenance-of-business work. If so, you and your team probably would benefit from performing those critical tasks at match play level rather than as a practice session. Practice sessions allow for stops, clarifications, discussion, while match play is done for the win. What might constitute a "win"? Setting a measurable goal. A measurable goal, such as completing a set of tasks within a specific time frame, or running a standard process with fewer than average defects, or splitting a group into two "teams" in competition with one another. All of these would help raise everyone's level of engagement.

And then there is time to goof off. Time for some levity!

No, we're not proposing that you encourage your employees to put their feet up and nap. Actually in some cultures this *is* encouraged. But, you should not only allow stress relief (fun), you should encourage it. All professionals, all hard working individuals, need to relieve stress – and you can't always wait until after the work day ends, nor should all "stress relief" occur at the local watering hole. Take the time to make work fun – or at least more enjoyable. We've seen organizations form teams to create internal entertainment. Sometimes these are official committees. Sometimes they're grass roots spontaneous "teams." In all cases though, leadership should welcome them and support them. A quick round of Nerf ball. A hallway "bowling tournament." A break room ping pong table. A parking lot Frisbee throw at noon. The possibilities are nearly limitless, and a few minutes of laughter and "goofiness" are priceless. Why do coaches appreciate seeing team members spend some time "goofing around"? Because it's NOT work. And because all interaction is communication. Every laugh not only reduces personal stress, but inter-personal tension as well.

Closing out the season: Developing a winning team

"Talent wins games, but teamwork and intelligence wins championships."
– Michael Jordan.

Ability + desire to learn + great attitude. These are the qualities every coach needs in her team. As we said at the beginning, a coach generally steps into an *existing* team environment. But no coach has to keep weak players, players who cannot learn effectively, or who simply will not learn because their attitudes short-circuit their potential.

Let's say this as succinctly as possible: team members have to be 100% in. Likewise, coaches cannot, must not, keep players who don't want to excel, don't have a desire to learn, *and* don't have a good attitude. No coach "owes" self-professed wanna-be's a spot on the team, and no coach should accept anything less than 100% effort at every practice and every scoring engagement. That means 100% of each individual's *effort*, not some mythical 100% "perfection." Everyone has off days. Everyone drops the ball sometimes. But a winning team means a team of winners, not a team of a few highly skilled talented people pulling along one or more malcontents. Each mistake is an opportunity to learn, and individuals learn best when their desire to do so is high. Same for an entire team – people learning and recognizing each other's skills and then learning to adapt symbiotically in ways to maximize total productivity requires a real desire to learn.

A great attitude is a powerful force. It appears automatically in a team that scores some wins, even if those wins are more accidental than earned. But a "great attitude" of feeling like a winner for a week or two pales in comparison to a great attitude through the rough times and hard work. Even a single great attitude on a team has a positive effect, but no amount of singular "rah rah" (from a player or a coach) can truly ignite a team. When a *team* has great attitude, positive energy is compounded, and people are so eager to improve that learning accelerates, causing abilities to improve faster than anticipated.

Wherever people must work together in any kind of grouping (sales teams, entire departments, after-hours bowling teams, etc.), positive attitudes help unite, while *great* attitudes resonate, unify, and ignite performance. If the coach is losing his great attitude, it's time for personal reflection and action. If a team member is displaying anything short of great attitude, the coach needs to point that out (publicly with respect, or privately based on the circumstance), and then demand the return of that great attitude. Skills can be taught, and abilities can improve. Desire to learn can grow as individuals realize progress. But great attitude is the "final mile," and is arguably the most visible attribute an individual demonstrates. There's a phrase psychologists use: "You cannot NOT communicate." All outward behavior is communication. And all communication (verbal and body language) loudly announces attitude.

"Pressure is what you feel when you don't know what's going on."
– Chuck Knoll.

Coaches, refine your teams! No player is guaranteed a "full season." Continually train your current players, but be on the look-out for new players who have (or have strong potential for) high achievement. Recruit, recruit, recruit. Do not hesitate to dismiss a weak player, even if their ability is above average but their attitude is not. Prove to your teams that you will stand by your mission, values, and goals. And most of all, remember – "coach" does not mean tyrant. Any fool can "command" a team to get out there and win. To coach is to lead, and from a broader perspective, to coach passionately is to build a passionate team!

Don't Manage...Coach!

So, you may have wondered when you started this book if we were serious. Perhaps we only want you to adopt *some* of the traits of a coach, act like a coach on occasion. Perhaps we were being metaphorical.

Well, if you didn't get the message from the previous pages – let us say in summation that we are not backing away from the concept of totally doing away with the management mind-set.

You manage things – not people.

If your most valued and valuable assets are your people, treat them that way.

We can learn more than a few tricks from sports coaches...we can use them as a model for how to create and maintain high-performing teams. We can learn to sustain a winning team.

Seriously.

Stop managing and start coaching!

References

On studying and learning from coaches.

The best way is to find coaches you admire and interview them. And of course that is nearly impossible. The coaches you'll admire are likely the ones you've seen on TV coaching your favorite professional team. There are other ways though.

Many coaches (college and professional) supplement their incomes through public speaking. It's not surprising that businesses bring in coaches to speak to their organizations. While working in the Office of Information Technologies for University of Notre Dame we had the special opportunity to listen to Coach Muffet McGraw speak to our unit. Besides the wisdom, she stayed and answered questions. A great lady who showed true humility. The opportunities are there.

Look for podcasts and video. Look for online archives of interviews of coaches.

And of course you can read their books. We read more than a few to provide references for this book. The trick is to ensure you're getting a book that has their theories and principles for building a winning team – not a book of memoirs. Publishers seek out any winning coach to write a new book. Win a world championship? Write a book. Win a National Championship? Write a book. Just because a coach wins doesn't mean she can transfer her wisdom via the written word. And it doesn't mean that the book they write will share the things that you need. So, read the reviews, the back cover, and the table of contents.

Here are few we can recommend.

Reach for the Summit: the Definite Dozen System for Succeeding at Whatever You Do, by Pat Summitt with Sally Jenkins. Random House, Inc., 1998

Courting Success: Muffet McGraw's Formula for Winning – in Sports and in Life, by Muffet McGraw with Paul Gullifor. Taylor Trade Publishing, 2003

Sacred Hoops: Spiritual Lessons of a Hardwood Warrior, by Phil Jackson and Hugh Delehanty. Hachette Books, 2006.

Players First: Coaching from the Inside Out, by John Calipari and Michael Sokolove. Penguin Books, 2015.

Winning Every Day; The Game Plan For Success by Lou Holtz. HarperBusiness, 1999.

Other books by the authors

Why Organizations Struggle So Hard To Improve So Little: Overcoming Organizational Immaturity by Martin Klubeck, Michael Langthorne, and Don Padgett. ABC-Clio, 2009.

Metrics: How to Improve Key Business Results by Martin Klubeck. Apress, 2011.

The Professional Development Toolbox: Unlocking simple truths by Martin Klubeck. 2014.

Planning and Designing Effective Metrics – abridged by Martin Klubeck, Apress, 2011.

54339852R00048

Made in the USA
Columbia, SC
30 March 2019